T0149366

VIEW from a Hillside

VIEW
from a
Hillside

ROBERT W. BARKER

VIEW FROM A HILLSIDE

iUniverse books may be ordered through booksellers or by contacting:

iUniverse
1663 Liberty Drive
Bloomington, IN 47403
www.iuniverse.com
1-800-Authors (1-800-288-4677)

ISBN: 978-1-5320-2023-0 (sc)
ISBN: 978-1-5320-2024-7 (e)

Print information available on the last page.

iUniverse rev. date: 04/11/2017

To two young lives, Hope and Elliot

who bring us light and treasure.

May your lives be full of love and kindness.

Foreword

These poems were written over several years. The reader will note that I still have a love for the shorter forms, inspired by the Japanese Haiku and Tanka styles of poetry. There is much to be said for the forced brevity of seventeen or thirty-one syllables, though modern Haiku and Tanka do not necessarily follow these rigid requirements. Nevertheless, in spite of my love for the rhythms of these short poems, I find myself gradually moving toward some longer forms. I hope you will find some enjoyment and meaning in this little book.

Contents

Tomorrow's Eyes

we are old, mother
though we don't believe it, not quite yet
we refuse the evidence
handed to us
so coldly

we still know we're young
thinking of tomorrow and beyond
though our view is shorter now
vision fading
a blessing

I watch the children
holding all tomorrow in their hands
swift and rippling laughter sings
chasing sunshine
still dancing

Dan and I

touching memories
old men will embrace bright snow;
playing children's games

The Met

aged and rusted
ancient sailors of velvet
tugged into place;
embracing the comforting
remembering boastful youth

Reunion

the room is full
overflowing noise
falling memories
remembered victories

we should not be
useless to all men
we have much to say
it still could be our day

we are cast off
husks of ripened grain
winnowed from the hay
our voices turned away

who still listens
to us?

Daniel

we connect again
so many miles, passing years,
we will slip away.
we touch the urgent moment
our bonds are not forever

Fading Memories

an old woman
       padding up the stairs
       in stocking feet

wondering where her living went
       softly passing by
       the picture of her husbands
       one by one

Robert W. Barker

Good Passage

touching many lives
the old man passes swiftly
grasping the moment;
he walks simply, confident
no regrets, no final fears

Faded Glory

whitest ghost
perched high upon the rocks
keep your history close
do not speak about your lovers
your creaking joints are hoarse from speaking
no one listens
no one hears you
your face a wreak of beauty lost
no paint will chase away that truth
turn away
look away
the storms will come, your days are numbered
I will leave you in peace
leave you and forget

(Summit House)

Robert W. Barker

Vultures

black wings stretch, reaching
cool morning, testing sun's warmth;
they assess my life

Legacy

bright sun promising
warm oak leaves sinking in snow
leaving life's image;
holding eternal fabric
I seek to imprint my soul

Robert W. Barker

Men of War

for some
there is no war
unloved;
but they do not send
their own sons

World United

new poisons
abound;
in the name of God
kill the strangers
save
their souls

Robert W. Barker

Hickory and Oak

the younger hickory
grows so straight behind the twisted oak
I will protect them both
serving ancient wisdom

an older hickory
down the hill among the oaks, so straight
there is real elegance
in unyielding straightness

they must speak, tree to tree
arguing the virtues of each form
I love them equally
measuring life's pathways

they're metaphor enough
for me

Burning Souls

fires burning brightly
the warring soul knows no peace
clashes with all life;
let us begin with soft words
eternity on our tongues

Headwaters

snow, quiet melting
water drops, tiny drum beats;
is this the ganga?

Remember

can we remember
the Holocaust?
can we remember
the countless, bloody genocides?
can we remember
all those who came before us on our lands?
can we remember
so many butchered human lives?

can we remember?
can we embrace the memory?

can we find
our soul?

Robert W. Barker

Marriage

under the shadow
cross shining in candlelight
blood red book held high;
beneath the bloody Christ
they speak their vows so softly

New York

the city of love
of primal lust and hatred
hopelessness and joy;
hard reflections capture me
I still feel your tattered soul

McCarthy

I have compassion for the men
that senseless drunkard would destroy
for petty indiscretions in their youth
has someone never been a fool
    when they were young?
they must have died before the agony of birth

the hunt still scurries on today
with hunters senseless as before
there is not one who can escape their wrath
and all of us are now the fool
    to listen close
so we may cringe at fractured lives and senseless pain

North to the Barrens

remember white vastness
bright, extending forever
beyond our hope
dreaming
see all the stars, our universe whole

remember emptiness
lonely and swallowed by God
searing our sight
striking
young hearts alive, filled with no fear

remember loneliness
feeling the land's still, soft breath
now without fear
shouting
standing on edge, heart filled with joy

remember bright lightness
heaviest burdens are lost
racing sharp wind
laughing
knowing no end, but happy youth

remember us young
remember us
young

Robert W. Barker

Arctic Dreaming

land of fierce sharp white wind
    shouting shrieking spirit
land of soft thick gray fog
    sentinel of silence

brilliant nights, blazing skies
    filled with blinding battles
days of still empty sight
    clear blue lakes lie waiting

rest alone, low black hills
    cold and long abandoned
lost in time endless sight
    far horizons taunt us

in the still morning light
    hear the earth speak clearly
by our ears whispers soft
    telling us her secrets

still we hear calls to us
    quietly insistent
secret soul here it lies
    only you can have it

Waiting for a Boy

across green valleys
chasing future memories;
he will bring his world

Robert W. Barker

Elliot's the Name

I know your name now
my little Elliot.
a wonderful name
Elliot Franklin Stone
it should serve you well

you like your first name?
I'll call you Elliot
or call you Franklin
or maybe call you Frank
if that's what you prefer

just at this moment
I see you are quite small
with a name that's grand
but I believe that you
will find it sized just right

one day

Young World

she knows no edges
walking calmly through them all;
who builds life's walls?

Robert W. Barker

Elliot's World

you look to see the world around
to see what we forgot
what we once saw
but cannot see
today

you build your world its future bright
creating what we lost
what we once built
but cannot build
today

the whole vast world around you, love
a love that we forsook
that love we knew
but do not know
today

you show us all we have strong hearts
strong hearts still, seeking hope
the hope we lost
that you'll help find
today

Night Messenger

softly between clouds
she passes white, impartial;
fracturing darkness

Robert W. Barker

Moon Rise

slow rise of an orange moon
piercing thin clouds on the cold night
reminding us of unchanging time

here on the side of Unquomonk
the black frontier, not so many years ago
who before me watched the moon rise
in sharp and bitter cold?
in the primal dark?

I can hear them calling me still
passing on the wind, faint and tiny voices
there is no protest, just a call
again reminding us
we are not the first

slow rise of the whiter moon
I do not fear whispered voices
they comfort me with quiet patience

Returning

sunlight cleaves darkness
ghosts of old friends take flesh;
twilight will intrude

Robert W. Barker

Fall Prophets

our little sumac
one scarlet shout at field's edge;
prophet of winter

Walking Down

still, snowy twilight
rose reflection to the east
snow clings to the oak

the nuthatch searching
for the last quick evening meal
scrambles head first, down

searching each crevice
in the black and rough-barked tree
busy and intent

a contrarian
with a different view of life
he finds his own way

he is a lesson
we should view life upside down
often, I believe

Robert W. Barker

Impatient

spring shivers in snow
dark trees hold red buds tightly
eagerness trembles;
this winter slowly yielding
teaches us soft patience

Birches and Calls

soft green
     reaching me, grasping, returning
across unnumbered years
     songs of a lost, sharp-edged youth

step back
     when did I walk pine-lined forests
losing and still finding
     working to become a man

I lost
     something I carried and left there
lost behind in green trees
     never to carry again

soft green
     effortless, carries me onward
memories still will return
     memories only, no more

Exaltation

now let there be spring
bright singing, lovers calling
in crackling sunshine;
cast off gray and silent age
exalting like long-tailed lambs

Loon Calls

calling
whistling, warbling, wavering
crossing the water in darkness

they hold a conversation
singing ancient songs

listen
wavering, whispering, whimpering
searing my heart through the forest

old memories rise to seize me
echoes from my past

hold me and help me remember

Robert W. Barker

Emerald Spring

emerald hills return
trees trumpet sharp, bright rebirth
ancient and forever;
window on eternity
come glimpse your own creation

It Will Be Gray

colors fade
the trees have let time pass
they will not stand against it
as we do

grand tall oaks
as wrinkled as old crones
their dressing limp and faded
as we are

all will wait
for Spring to be refreshed
the trees will stand quite naked
as we will

one more Spring
perhaps just one more Spring
enjoy the crisp bright winter
as we should

Striptease

my oak undresses
slowly, shyly, teasing me
I must be patient;
she will perform on her time
stark naked in mid-winter

Four Toms

four young toms
strut, display their strength
    their beauty
    their male attraction

no young hens
stand by to watch them
    their showing
    their self-absorption

they practice
their living dances
    for the rut
    their reason for life

four young toms
hoping soon to dance
    do they know
    we all are waiting?

Robert W. Barker

Winter's Darkness

snow falling softly
wind rattles dry black branches
mute deer stand waiting;
cold suns will set too quickly
darkness settles on our souls

Lost Viewpoint

the valley is lost today
hidden in the fog below the sun
waiting through invisibility
I know it lies there
but it will not speak to me
I cannot hear its brightness
nor see its noisy banter
but through the thinning fog
I still can touch those many souls
in my restless mind

Robert W. Barker

Winter Vision

warm days vanish
colors dim to black and white;
edge of brittle time

Morning Gossips

the early morning gossips
all screeching with each other
their raucous harsh complaining
and aimless flight and mutter
always brings them comfort

quickly parting, swiftly flying
making all their daily choices

do they decide the place and time
for the end of day reunion
to gather all their wild relations
to make their day worth living?

with all their noise and bluster
crow's family functions better
than most that I have known

Awakening

bird song insistent
morning is here, here, here, here;
I will sleep no more

Spring Songs

swamps will live out loud
life springs in wild explosions
nature's effusions;
but what I have created
will it sing and jump for joy?

Winter Perfection

snow touches the night
a breathless soft redemption;
frozen perfection

Close Encounter at Borestone

she slides silently
smoothly across rounded pebbles
through short tufts of grass

two tiny frogs
leap as one into the shallow pond

she does not follow
pausing only a moment
she slides softly into taller grass

and she is gone

Last Leaves

at last sumac leaves
fragment black roads with color
fall's triumphal march;
winter follows, no fanfare
all announced in black and white

Swamp Maples

earliest criers
ringing sharp bells of color;
our season changers

Robert W. Barker

American History?

shall our history now be made
by anger, shouts and useless noise
by those who will believe that they should lead
by those who latch upon the fears
of all the ignorant
of the mass of fools
of those who are afraid
by those who raise the fearful specters
of the racist
of the sexist
of the fascist
of the Nazi
they are themselves the grandest nightmare
they raise the darkest bile
of our worst natures

Hyannis Son

we pay him homage
our young man of memories
the myth maker;
beneath the handsome son
shimmering golden shadows

Embrace

some of us are angry
some have been angry forever
some of us are lonely
some have been lonely forever
some of us are fearful
some have been fearful forever
some of us are in pain
some have been in pain forever

can we feel the anger?
can we feel loneliness?
can we feel fearfulness?
can we feel the sharp pain?
in those we do not understand?
we must not fear the rich embrace

Empty Heart

my heart is empty
I fear divisions
my arms reach
to fill my heart

I reach for happiness
I find bitterness
I reach for hope
I find despair

what is happening?
where is the desire?
the good future
for all of us?

I want our empty hearts
to beat together
to work as one
for tomorrow

can our empty hearts
gorge on our dreams
bright and shiny
for tomorrow?

Robert W. Barker

People of the Fear

we are the people of the fear
we are afraid
    of the darkness
we are afraid
    of the cold wind
we are afraid
    of strong currents
we are afraid
    of religions
we are afraid
    of our dying
we are afraid
    of everything

I reject the call of all our fears
standing firm in the darkness
    I will face the black night
standing firm on the mountain
    I will face the fierce wind
standing firm in the river
    I will face the wild current
standing firm in the hatred
    I will face our many gods
standing firm in my living
    I will face my pending death
standing firm to savor life
    I will face my own future

The City of Red

Paris, the joyful city of light
is now the city of our fears
the city of our joy, of culture and our love
is now the city of our blood
our blood flows freely in the streets
the center of the least of all our fears
has now become the city of the red

we are in shock the people say
the people say that we must mourn
that sudden loss of joy and love
but those in power will not mourn
we are at war, they say, we must attack
and kill some other blameless souls
their blood must now anoint our dead

one blood-red river joins another
with bodies ground to senseless dust
close the borders, close the mosques
let all the refugees be damned
must all our joy and kindness die?
must all now drown in waves of blood?
joyful Seine now running red

we'll join together hand in hand
and then we will destroy... ourselves

Robert W. Barker

Dark Wind

there is a wind
blowing darkly
across the landscape of our souls

it burns our hearts
leaving cinders
where once lived smiles and silver bells

we weep, we cry
cursing dark winds
but only fools will fight the dark

raise white sails
and fly

World Trade Center

standing stiff I touch a name
feeling names unknown to me
rubbing gray unyielding stone;
hearts were broken, mine was not

I remember standing there
watching, shaking disbelief
nearly naked standing still
freezing in my fear of loss

reach him touch him hold my son
snatch him back alive and whole
silence greeted all my calls
standing now I feel old fear

coming home he smiled at me
full of youth he cried, no fear
some would wait for smiles unseen
hearts were broken, mine was not

Robert W. Barker

Family Spirits

once the box is opened
those family spirits rise like smoke.
my great-grandfather rises first
he was so depressed, he killed himself
two days before his daughter's wedding date
she must have had some unkind words
how inconsiderate, but carry on
the wedding should go on as planned
it would be a shame for all these guests
to have to travel twice
when they're already here

Waiting for Her

sitting in silence
deafened by my restless mind;
no words within reach

Fierce Love #2

we awake each morning
attached by old familiarity
so long a time as one

she has stood beside me
held me when I would have fallen
picked me up again when I did
we have lingered close together many years
she has stayed when it would have been so easy
to have left

I can be so full of trouble
for those who love me
I know this all too well

she knows my fears and darkest secrets
yet still she holds me close
and I have said before
there is no right to love
this fierce

Stranger

she a forlorn stranger in his life
    so quiet, sadly still
though he welcomes her with happy smiles
    she still remains morose
weren't you happy once before? He asks
    today I can't recall
but... we laughed and shouted once
    do you forget my tears?
truly you were happy, joyful then
    I wept. You never heard
shouts of joy concealed your hidden pain?
    consumed by your desire
god forgive me; did I ever know?
    we will forgive us both

Porcupine

white branches shining,
stripped bare by our spiny friend;
his is a cold meal
in the snow I forgive him;
it is his garden, not mine

Morning too Quickly

morning rushes in upon us fiercely
thin fog mixed with wood smoke
softly rises from the narrow valley
too slow, sun shouts, and makes its harsh demands
face the day, and rise, young fool
make yourself a man, again, and quickly

your impatience is not welcome here, sun
do not wake me harshly
not from the slumber of the nearly dead
I must insist on slower starting days
like the cat I curl myself
lying warm, beside the barren window

I will purr

Robert W. Barker

Emily of Amherst

she quivers on edge
a dancing ghost, transparent;
bound in enigma

By Right

she was there by right
in the darkness she was there ahead of me
and her ancestors
they have lived here many generations
many more than mine
compared to her
I have arrived only yesterday

it was much too late
I saw her in the darkness but much too late
and I heard her strike.
I shouted, paused, and drove on to my home
still I do regret
not going back
the next day there was no sign of her

an inconvenience
for me no more than simple inconvenience
her? perhaps her death

Robert W. Barker

Anna Bolena

the ancient queen has come alive
her voice can pierce the ages
she wants us all to notice
    and I do

dead for some five hundred years
her resurrected visage brings
endless cheers, applause and shouts
    and our joy

it is an ancient story full of blood
of treachery and betrayal
but holding love and bravery
    as it must

I stand with all the rest and cheer
as curtains fall and rise again
it's nothing more than history
    well sung

Travel Day

start the day
slowly
trees embracing byways
quiet, ancestral
winding, hidden

end anxious
racing
wide and barren highways
filled with angry noise
harsh, demanding

all seek tomorrow

Robert W. Barker

One Room

They built for running children;
the simple farmers raised the walls
and formed the single open room
then built two privies, one each side.
They built for futures each one dreamed
but never dreamed the future now.
They built it for a thriving town
where children ran and laughed aloud
where air still overflowed with sound
and all the pungent smells of farms
and all the sweat of simple men
still autographed the mid-day breeze.

The oaks and birch displace the hay,
and trees replace the berry patch.
I cannot hear the children run;
the tiny school still stands, forgot
so shrunken by encroaching oaks.
The noisy students all are still;
they've vanished to the city's weft.
Those few who lived their summers here,
they all have moved to brighter dreams.
I listen to the silent shade,
to shouts of children ever lost,
and feel the growing autumn chill.

Mind Rain

twenty years too parched
lost in deserts of the mind;
now see falling rain
washing thoughts away to die
mourning still their passage